HEARTWRECKS

poems by

Nicolas Destino

Alexander, Arkansas
www.siblingrivalrypress.com

Heartwrecks

Cover photograph by Kathleen Farrell. Used by permission.

Author photograph by Seth Ruggles Hiler. Used by permission.

Cover design by Bryan Borland.

Sibling Rivalry Press, LLC
13913 Magnolia Glen Drive
Alexander, AR 72002

www.siblingrivalrypress.com
info@siblingrivalrypress.com

ISBN: 978-1-937420-35-2

Library of Congress Control Number: 2012951647

First Sibling Rivalry Press Edition, February 2013

for Seth

in arrivals

in departures

HEARTWRECKS

in arrivals

Resurrection

Back in the city they were erecting the moon every night with ropes, pulling, as everything needed to rise to reverse what fell. In an upstate kitchen, amid the languid, flat dough, they got the news that there would be no more bread, not until the moon was back up and pulling of its own accord.

Broadcast

That morning I was a husband, a maker of fried eggs and Sunday fruit, an integral part of my neighborhood, drinking coffee with heaven mirrored on its surface, and my imagination cast out to the oiled sky.

I drank the coffee to drink it away and to be a harmless partaker in neighborhood mechanics, waiting, like everyone, for the next moment, to be tolerated, rolling out of Jersey City, toward towns of prairies or prairies of towns, depending on which direction, depending on the escaper you ask.

To be plain, like everyone, hearing the voice of god, and to feel human and unfantastic, like everyone in the next apartment and the next apartment next to the next apartment, being tolerated and turning on radios broadcasting the voice of god, waiting for the next moment with all the escapers living inside of it.

Palimpsest

If today you find yourself deleted from the map drive invisibly toward the office of urban planning despite the centuries of names already established for you. Continue to undo all the completions; just remove the asphalt from the street and the street from the dirt, undo the equation of the street name linked to the image of a dangerous neighborhood, put back the horses and the beginning before you were called anything, and do this silently behind your eyes from the office window, looking upon your marvelous reconstruction as today this is your best option.

Viva-

You were always rain drips translated to pizzicato
and I adored you instantly.

Today when I was not writing poetry,
asleep at the desk with an apple next to my head,

dreams told me that tiny violinists can hide anywhere
inside apples, inside dreams of apples and not

inside sleeping heads of other violinists in Venice.
They told me it was enough to adore anyone

through his translation whether he is rain drips
or the imaginary songs apples make inside dreams,

anyone.

Healing Process

My digestive system works better if I eat this type of yogurt
one year after his funeral I don't bother to use a spoon
just let it reach room temperature and somewhat drink it
from the cup.

Switch

All of us vertical and compressed on the downtown train heading toward the midnight version of New Jersey full with the shadows of immediate futures, there, laying claims from one hand to the next, all simplified by an old woman wrapping her arms around my waist to keep from tipping as the train bubbles under water waking me up in the body of someone else's husband.

The Conductor Is Waiting

I want to give you places. Your apartment comes with fists and oven grease. You look for objects shining out of music and count along the meters. You can find yourself waiting for synchronisms, aligning your exits.

I want to give you places. You can go there alongside the cellists, their autumn trees between their knees, and try to find the objects they are missing, activate their arms to motion. The conductor is waiting. You can find yourself waiting.

Indigenous

Miraculous to be part of the snow globe with the penguins
on the icebergs and the icebergs with the cold shock and
miraculous to be inside the dome with the curvature of
the dome and the penguins' heads and the cold shock far
from the city where this is not taking place and to be apart
from the towers and a part of interiors with the curve of
the moon made from clay.

Maintenance

In a store, on a cell phone
she clutched a coke
from a warm angry cooler
all matter ready to burst
but the clerk breathed back winter
filling her lungs
blowing a chill back
into the afternoon
back into the cooler.

Oil on Canvas

Every night if a figure appears in your bedroom
doorway, tall and glowing blue, scratched into the scheme
that you're not sleeping alone, then what?

If the image of a figure arrives, there are fantasies,
born on the doorstep of a tulip, the rhetoric
of fitting inside the frame of another man,
blooming you into muscled sleep until you
wake up more masculine than before.

The Pines of Rome

Opaque and often bound opal
over pastoral elegiac flow
overt with ostracized oboes
in the hands with contaminate blow
oeuvre of order and Ottorino Respighi
obelisk in the Pines of Rome
out of order in pasture and contaminate blow
in the obelisk Pines of Rome.

Tempest

In my version of your Storm at Sea,
the water settles itself to murmurs
after turbulent treble settles the sand
dollars and lobsters back on the floor
just as we settle when we are exhausted
by furious and gorgeous swells.

In my version of your Storm at Sea,
I am trundled in a waterspout among
vital electric threads of green and spindled
up the tunnel to rushes of sixteenth notes,
then we all fall down, down the spout
onto the tonic seabed back to sanctuary.

Delicate Aches

For boys who carve their images in water,
always shifting into ripples of faces
then back to water, let there be boys
who will let them be boys outside the image
of boys, no matter what distortions are found
in rippling mirrors, and let them be boys
who will know what their own faces
will look like in armfuls of years into
the future, the simple future with real mirrors.

Proposition

My tie looked off-center, a pedestrian misplacement, purple silk in the wrong angle, not quite ready for the suit. I step out into the world despite offhanded slanted things, but today it is all steam and rocky terrain, barren where my neighborhood was, and a gentleman suited in fine gray wool comes out of mist asking to join me on my walk to work, or to the expectation of where we would end up.

I Had a Hammer

Hours, please, bring happy, bring things, things,

it's a thing, it's a recliner, it's just a staircase made shorter, yes?

Bring the simples for sampling of little morsels on platters.

Hours, I expect a phone call to bring me rings

and bring me nails or the opposite hand of a carpenter

reaching to me, dropping tools

I was looking for,

and by the end of the day I'll climb stairs

that is all, that is all, that is all.

Impersonal Ad

The you that I crave is not far away
on a tilted antenna
on tip of the octopus
on outstretched tentacle
not far away
be it said I'm the craver
and not far away on a train
lodging outcasts en route to the you
who is not far away
who is hungry and bearlike
who is obstinate bed-hog
who is weaver of signals
for a craving cartographer
not far away.

Yet

Safe because it may not happen safe
as in I am safe and we are safe
in safety for the sake of not being kicked
also because they did not know I loved him
before he was kicked in sacred places just as I
first noticed   first noticed
the future driving to safety in a red car
toward the sun toward a savior and there is light up there
just as they say   just as they say
up there in the hungry atmosphere where it has not happened
there where didn't where not where I loved him will be said
for the first time in safety before kicked before saying I loved
him
not yet.

Sleep Therapy

Things like giraffes, that's all, and catalogue items, ordinary things; driving in the snow in the repetitive shapes of snowflakes, and things like fruit markets and police activity activating the amalgams of scriptures inscribing all the checklists that qualify a city, but the real story is the flashing number eight in a waiting room, outside of which people have held doors in restaurants for strangers, or have stolen their pocket books or parking spaces, or have let doors slam on strangers, but the real story is that I would give up all these dirty thoughts for healthcare.

Party Mishap

Prelude had turned everything to ice.
The staircase, if you will, signaled their arrivals.
But if you won't, it signaled a frozen staircase
and the option of slipping down.

In the composer's notebook it stated
E major as the right key to create ice,
especially at night, when expectation
hammered their hearts upon arriving.

The prelude stated that one should
expect more, if you will, guests in peacock
costumes. But if you won't, just peacocks
gliding up the staircase or slipping down.

Essay on Baroque Ornamentation

(to be spoken rapidly)

It begins with this music I describe as curly, much like the sound of cuckoos. The thing making the music I describe has no relation to cuckoos. The thing making the music I describe is not a bird, but strings stretched over wood. Another musician arrives to ask what I describe as the curly music much like the sound of cuckoos, but having no relation to cuckoos.

I tell the other musician who arrives that I describe the curly music much like the sound of cuckoos as cuckoos because there are two notes, one higher one lower, like the cuckoos'. The other musician who arrives describes the two notes of the cuckoo, one higher one lower, as a minor third, and suddenly there are intervals, and suddenly there is articulation of these things.

The other musician who arrives describes the two notes of the cuckoo, one higher one lower, as a minor third in either direction, but out of the context of cuckoos and into the context of Bach and immediately there is articulation of *these* things. The articulation of *these* things leads to the articulation of the stick that strokes the strings stretched over wood, using horse hair, but having less relation to horses, and more relation to Bach.

The other musician who arrives describes the many ways to articulate the notes of Bach, one higher one lower, like the cuckoos, but with better technique to make a curlier music. The other musician articulates the difference in structure between the notes of Bach and the notes of the cuckoos, one higher one lower, in the baroque and rococo eras, and speaks of techniques to articulate the stick that strokes the strings stretched over wood to make a curlier music, and immediately there is articulation of *these* things, and the other musician describes *these* things, much not like the thing making music with strings stretched over wood, much not like curly, much not like the sound of cuckoos, one higher one lower, much not at all.

The Inversion

A boy was a shark. A man was a minnow.
There is still work to be done here.

Sometimes they have to live expeditiously,
to be the fastest fish,
      to be champion in this way.

Take anger out on the water. In the gills
that filter it. There is work to be done here.
A boy swaps with a man.
      They think they are champions in this way.

Short Story

Having yanked out the lights mid story
a man asked a man, what is a torpedo?

It wasn't that they're sad.
It wasn't.
The sun simply dipped away.
It did.

A man said to take all the time you need
in flesh and definition.

Wait for the light.

It wasn't that they were asleep.
A torpedo scraped along the sky without a word.

It did.

Painting a Zebra

If the cello sweeps along the corner of an ear, then let the cello. If the ice cube melts along letters of the book cover, then let the ice cube. If the woman who loves the woman in apartment 3B brings her up a bowl of hot cello music, then let the ice cube melt along the bowl's ridge, and let the bowl sit half empty in the kitchen of apartment 3B, and let the book cover the eyes of the woman who brought the bowl of hot music as she naps on the sofa in apartment 3B, and let this be the way the evening evaporates.

Maestrofont

My dearest Vivaldi, how I miss you, with
larks leaving at the right time
opening curtains for the next season in a
set of four.
You ask of my toes as they begin to numb;
something drastic is
on its way—
your *internal fire*, but for now you're secretly
kissing archdukes long ago, then my toes,
but for now these four snowflakes on my
fingertip,
evenly spaced in this ordered formation,
each a tiny chime of A major,
can be rearranged.
See what happens when I move the
rightmost snowflake to the left?
The chord is inverted—now I have been
dead for centuries
while today you are just being born.

BWV 1064

We are dancing in and out
of doors in voluptuous cheer.

Creator is a mystery.

This susurrus of three violins
puzzles together

the danger of turning into fiddles.

Bach knew what he was doing;
for a minute we again believe in god.

In Love

It wasn't known if the ship's men arrived today as heartwrecks, nor was it known if they arrived in love with other men away from ships. When one man held the twitching lobster in the fireball glow of autumn evening, he looked sad, but it wasn't known if he arrived as wrecked, arrived as an ornament in the fireball glow, arrived as a twitching lobster, it wasn't known if he arrived at all.

Technicolor

for Tyler Clementi

I once had a million or more friends
from the view on the bridge.
Faceless heads among the colors
of the towers, and the colors of
towers turning to pink under
light blocking sky puffs above
the blocks of faceless heads
that were my millions of friends
from the view on the bridge.

Colors became necessary, a sign
hung on the bridge said so.
When the sky puffs moved
to let back the light, my million friends
turned into colorful balloons
because it was not so simple,
this transformation, heads to balloons,
all floating upward to meet me
on the bridge by the sign that said so.

Object Lesson

If it actually was a pterodactyl flying in curves around the sun, you have seen a terrific day. If it or if it not, no matter, it was still a terrific day of curving dances and brightness out there even if you have seen the imitation of a pterodactyl.

Myth

Your arms weren't satisfied stretching
with nothing in them
to stretch, or embracing only their likeness,
so I gave you
a horsetail. In the daytime
there were sheep I slaughtered to turn
their insides into chords,
and the daytime sheep-chords relieved
you of your ears poked by chirping bats,
and taxi cabs and wholly
the echelon of noisemakers
in the night. All I assembled
together appeared as a stick of hair
and a body of chords,
which then I placed inside your arms,
asked you to pull the hair
across the chords until you
found the desired sound.

Genesis

And you by the pond, pre-thruway, counting ducks, plural then back to zero. How many you are, among innumerable twigs having become other kinds of sticks, let's say toothbrushes, let's say drinking straws, for eventually I should build a house to house innumerable things I could never contain, then smile, smile big, then bigger for the photograph where joy is entombed, because this is a beginning of all joy, then joys, where first you, and then you plural, were spotted by the pond, pre-thruway, working your way back to zero, then our zero, and equal to our clear landscape.

Intimate Hoarding

Contamination is one. Contaminations are many. Check to see if the water is dirty. I know. There will be a time when there is a leak while we caress. There will be a time while loving when something dirty washes out from the river and into the front yard. There was a time when I didn't know the word yard, a time when you didn't know caressing.

Books, shoes, bottles, forks, bags, cups, tires. Tonight we will have chocolate cake. All of this has washed up to our door. After the news, there is a time when we are unsure. After the cake, there is time for sleep. After the news, the books, bottles, forks, plastic bags, cups, tires, cake, the sleep, there is a time to say we already knew, but there isn't any edge to scrape these away. We keep snuggling quietly among our collections, piling our bodies in contact. I know.

in departures

Out Love

It wasn't known if the truckers departed toward or away from husbands, nor was it known if their sunburns or blistered cargo held the maps, but the crates loosened flocks of parrots. One trucker held an emerald bird vibrating under the hot red bubble before departing, but it wasn't known if the trucker departed toward a husband, toward emerald parrots, or toward dreams of arrivals, and as the red heat evaporated everything, it wasn't known if the trucker departed at all.

Ghetto Vocalise

There are no bright drops
of music in this homeland,
no opera, no Othello in its lungs,
but sometime ago I expected
provisions of other bodies to hold,
instead a universe was built
out of household objects, plastics
in the shaking night
once said to replace tremolo
when there are no violins
and violins once said to replace
a body for shaking
once said to replace the dry homeland
with bright drops of music
and a body I could sing to life
with the name, Othello.

Sleeping with Darwin

Oh, absence of speaking, and brittle starfish,
and life form in my bed I cannot name, and feral
earth of origins, where can we begin?

Oh, Galileo and his rightness of those
sparkling twinklers, and hangover city of lovers
in loverships and sexual variations

with the life form in my bed I cannot name, and the history
of Beethoven pounding away in all the tonal
variations, where can we begin?

And the life form in my bed I cannot name in lovership,
his right angle upon me, and something forced,
and myself split in two,
and the suddenness of becoming two things.

Assimilation

The leaf sifter slowed her search for the leaf
with the clearest resemblance to elation,
however that would appear in touchable form.

The yellow sky poured down more leaves
onto her diminishing pile where she found
that each leaf was no more than a simple
innovation on a theme of another.

The sifter flattened her body into a small
five-pointed shape with a blazing red hue
folded up there in elation of no other choice.

Stand Partner

My arm is your arm. Your book is my book.
Our waltz is their waltz. Your three is my four.
These bows are our bows. Not theirs but our bows.
Your elbow's my bow. My elbow's your bow.
Your lin is my vio. My vio your lin.
You beg when I'm in. You're in when I beg.
We beg when we're in. Begin.

Outcome

At orchestra rehearsal, at accidental time,
at January bluster,
the back of your head with haloed glow,
we practice divine departures
when it's over, the way the taxi or train door closes, closes
the aperture of your f-hole
beaming when your violin tilts just so,
closes, closes, taking all the vibrato home,
closes the aperture
of January inside your beaming f-hole.

American Cookies

They were all sleeping at once in the
same house

in every permutation of sleeping,
and they were neatly organized into
their own beds, like socks in
drawers, and every permutation of
socks in drawers, including cotton
bolls sleeping in the drawers of the
fields, and this was the house of
gentle breathing, especially when
visitors said
this is the way it should be, you're doing
things right.

They were all proud in their
rightness of being right, in right
angles under the red roof of the
house, with the right recipe for
frosted cookie moons, and especially
the light way they breathed and
moved around each other in the
house when
another slept.

But the good and right ways of
sleeping changed when socks in
organized drawers, and every
permutation of order, including

recipes for frosted cookie moons
were rearranged, and visitors said
this isn't the way it should be, you're
doing things wrong.

They were all sleeping at once in
different houses.

Light

Without it you're less a painter, painter of cheetahs, cheetahs are less themselves and more interpretations of spots, spots that hearken back, back to a canvas where there was nothing, nothing could have been so bright, bright as the premier of an intelligent animal, animal like me and you, you sitting at the convergence of beginnings, beginning a phrase in a painting, painting a turn, turning around to my face, lighting the lamp, the lamp we have to extinguish before long, long into the sleep where I held you, painter of cheetahs, painter of cheetahs, where I turned off the lamp to find only interpretations of ourselves.

Doors & Chambers

Latin drum beats in apartment C
Mozart in Apartment E
at night the drums at day the strings
at night the sway of day brittle winds
and all is quiet quite in the hall of the mountain king.
We descend the steps to check our mail in boxes marked
by suffixes, passing each other up and down the steps in
relative key of quietude then back to beats for one and
back to trills eventually tumbling over the precipice of
steps in rhythmic inconsequence of correspondence.

A Spacesuit Can Save You

Because there was a glitch in your travel plans you need to reenter the earth's atmosphere without searing up, to hear once more that you're in a safe place whether it's a carnival of glassmakers blowing crimson orbs, or a carnival of animals, or of one antelope in a safe place, where words are organized and properly published by a carnival of publishers who can place your sexuality in books your family will never open, because there was a glitch in your family's travel plans, rerouting them to other carnivals instead of places of pagination, and that is one very happy family riding away on an antelope in the opposite direction.

Homeless

Stranger, I am sorry for making eye contact with you. In my defense, I was alone when you passed before me without irises, stranger, this is serious, we are no longer the same. While it began about you, stranger, entirely about you, you saw me too and I was this dreadful war someone had covered in winter wool. Stranger, I am a coat! Imagine this day inverted you into the womb. Imagine emerging from a new mother or a brick building upon the sidewalk. You can't fool me, stranger, our eyes are the planets within where we rotate.

Travelogue

In my passenger captivity I am partnered in a Chrysler
passing and passing the ersatz planets
                    or glowing discs high up on poles
furnished by gas stations
in dreams of lighting the way for greater travels
even in blizzards.

We speak as companions about heat
finding our source of hands inside flamed spaces
wishing our insides to be as luminous as the real stars
in real travel
in real language
all along our drive toward some other and real
kind of planet.

They Send in Dreams

Let's build a canary from scratch, you and me, in a puddle, testing the efficacy of simple, from a condo in the keys, not for you not for me, not the alligator sex we planned, not the birds, not their awesome equivalence, not the loans in forbearance, not the letters in the loans or the senders of the letters with canaries spinning around their heads, not for you and not for me, not that simple, give me the keys to that borrowed roller skate, not the leased vehicle, and not the actual building of a canary, just the efficacy of hallucinations, not anything but the concept of let's build, not for you not for me but forbearances in letters where a puddle ought to be.

Snow Globe

Once there was a blue ball.

Cotton fields were dropped upon it.

Fire fields were dropped upon it.

Water fields, multiplication and division tables
were dropped upon it too, then chairs to sit and figure
the proper boundaries of these.

Colorful wanderers were dropped upon it.

Thoughts were dropped within the clouds
dropped inside their heads while sounds

were dropped inside their thoughts

all coming alive.

Sunday Morning

When you live alone you can put things where you wish.
Alone, you can contaminate your own environment and
spill olive oil on an orange floating in the sink. You can
sink where you want to, in your own particles, part the
water in your own sink, create miracles. You can say
excuse the mess... would you like a drink? When you live
alone you are naked more often. If another man is naked
with you in bed, you can say *welcome visitor.* If another
man contaminates your environment, you can say *thanks
for coming over,* and you can clean up after him with old
rags only you know where to find.

Fantasy

for Jeffrey

We loved wind so much that
we talked about buying kites.
When we finally bought
kites, we continued to talk
about flying them
on windy days.

We talked about disasters,
where the kites would tangle
into wind, how far into
things we loved, upward and
away from the sticky beach.

When we reviewed all
possible outcomes for
disasters, we went there, to
the sticky beach, with our
kites, to the boardwalk where
a sign alerted us that all wind
was cancelled until we were
ready to lose one another.

Trajectory

A diagram in a book by the metronome agrees with perfection drawing its antagony on the next page through trembling depictions of comets interspersed with errant commas, say collisions, and suns flaring the wrong light for their temperatures. Then all ticks back to order on the following page with images moved into their own quadrants, as it is when one of us moves into another room, closing the door.

False Alarms

At just the right temperature we can expect
to hear bells from chapels of heat. Smoke will
signal something dire or trite, but meticulous
in the intensity of one or the other.

There will be a moment when we choose
to stand still, a moment when we run wild
toward landscapes of extreme conditions.
There will be a moment when choosing
is absurd.

Separation Anxiety

Someday there will be goals of bending into the shape of paper clips but for now your knees only fold in one direction. Someday his lips won't taste so metallic and he'll ask you to be the object in the line unfolded from a sheet of paper. Someday you'll stand in front of a mirror framed in fire and he with less metallic lips will sneak up behind you direct and objective and you'll begin a reevaluation of accomplishments.

The Gardeners

Today I want to plant homonyms and equations between silver rows of allegro flowers. But the truth is there's nothing here. You can see evidence in the acts of other gardeners. They come to this plot, their hands wringing life from trumpet vines only because they are thriving. Notice how the blood of trumpet vines isn't quite as red as ours. Notice how other things begin to grow in their place. Permit yourself to sing a little.

Like you I would begin in major keys

The enclosures around us prevent unfortunate slips into the wrong species of counterpoint, animal, all. One composer had to build tropical fish in a musical image, give them temporary legs to step out of the aquarium for touches of something otherworldly. We are not so brave.

Expedition

They had their own quests for beautiful.
Some went to stores for purple fabrics, curly maples.
Some went north for narwhal heads, spirals,
entire heads cut off just for one twisting tooth.

Score Falls Swiftly off the Stand

Your understanding begins in C major,
which is a good place to start,
not actually a place
but a variation of another key
or the relative key of A minor.
Now the understanding moves
toward aberrant thoughts of words
like "Secaucus" or "Tortoise"
exactly at the point where Bach ended
the phrase, and this is good, you want
phrases, to be a complete statement,
to understand that even the geography
is about the sonata, uninterrupted
even by the bell, which turns out to be
your imagination of the bell, then reaching
the door where there is no one, or the door
becomes a portal to Saturn where broken
violins go to rest, where thoughts of aberrant words
have some relationship to "sonata"
and the understanding moves toward desire,
which is not a place but just a variation
of things you don't want.

Concerto Gross in D Major op. 6, no. 4

It's much like framework to say heaven is emerald and endless lawns above and to the right, where composers like Archangelo Corelli are held hostage. It's much like framework to say heaven is a winter night just below the prostate gland, where sense memory is held hostage to the sounds of a Corelli string work. It's much like framework to say that heaven is ladders going above and to the right of your sense memory, when put into words resembles emerald lawns in winter, crystallizing to the rhythm of a Corelli string work. Then everything held hostage is released at the same time.

Labyrinth

Whether it's the edge or the center of the map becomes unstable as you roll along its black surface, much the way you are as a marble freewheeling on the concave then convex surface of the map that was meant to be of the oceans but is a map of stars even though sperm whales are there with you where they don't belong in the stars rolling around much the way we roll around when we are marbles on a waving surface looking for something like a nook or an alternate body of water.

Artifact

You're free to leave at any time. Freedom. There is still a trace of Tupperware in my mother's cupboard from a phase of themed social gatherings back in the eighties. All the guests have gone, free to go, but imprisoned in the moment where it's orange and waxy. You want to go someplace too, unlike a chamber with a warped lid, or inside the cupboard itself into another phase of themes, but with the understanding that you are much less durable than the remnants found there.

Antecedent

A flaw is born in the second time I call your name. I will leave out the details of all excess identity. On the avenue, any avenue, with throngs of goers dressed in snowflakes, everyone a snow-flaked head, then what? If not for the hardship in placing you with amorphous and cold goers on any avenue, I would forget the rapture of calling your name.

If no, then yes, but where?

In the meadow I don't have, love me. In addition, by the time weeds and words become wordweeds sprouting out pavement breaking apart tar, love me by then. I've already said that, though not in the meadow I don't have, not by the time the... and the time the... not in addition to anything, and certainly not by the time the tar and the time the pavement, but surely by the time it takes to rearrange words and weeds to seeds and swords, or in the love I have, don't meadow me.

But plainly, in the meadow, breaking up the tar and pavement, I've already said that, though not with the addition of seeds, because the meadow is not what I have, and love me is not what I have, but something in addition to a disaster is rearranging weeds to words, clutching the pavement, surely by this time it takes additional tar, and certainly by this time I've already said that, love me, by this time a meadow is breaking.

Habitual Pasture

This winter everything will be better.
The harbingers of music will all be there,
we'll have new wool suits for the circle
of the buffalo and the owls that will all be

the harbingers of music, always there.
This winter everything will be better
for the buffalo and the owls and the elk,
and for us in our new wool suits listening

to them, the harbingers of music always there,
inflecting the notes of the songs in the voice.
This winter everything will be better.
We will sit gathered and loved and warm,

with the buffalo and the owls and the elk
perfecting our songs in the snow,
all of us in our new wool suits, listening,
singing, as harbingers of music always there.

Polyphony
for Hannah P. (1985-2010)

When Hannah caught a terrible case of the fugue, she
slept with bottles of elixirs on her pillow, trying to cure
her voice, now speaking in harmonies, but little could be
done outside of constructing an environment of ladders,
and to escape this, to escape this room, to escape this new
room in many directions, to escape this room at different
elevations with different voices, to say from the space
above to the space below, I escaped *that* space, from the
ladders, one tilted this way, one tilted that, in all the new
openness while the sunset gave vertical clouds in upward
sweeping strokes, a sky full of ladders angled toward the
pink fire, she feels complete in the harmony of her new
and several selves.

Shift

As in
one thing to the other

As in
you had a meadow now you don't,
had a winter or an apartment, had blues
not as azure as before,
as azure as before,
azure as before,
as before.

How things diminish in duration.

Our love is printed in arrivals and departures, in lobsters
and sun, dancers awaiting truckers,
flights of green reptiles and fish on borrowed legs, as if to
say right now and not yet.

This duration, majestic and obscene, this duration

of gifts
for you!

As in
one thing to the other.

As in
the intimacy of riding a giraffe or an antelope to the
hospital
for immediate care.

As in
curving pink towers, slanted from the version
in the snow globe,
the version broadcasted to neighborhoods in cities
where sometimes there is a prairie
right now and not yet,

not for you
not for me

but for the time it takes to run out of light,
that orange lamp we turn off
at night when the room forgets our faces.

As in an angry customer freewheeling like a marble on
surfaces of maps, always leaving, grasping blue figures in
doorways, one thing to another, because all exist together
in arrival and departure, but there
in the love we have and don't, there is this trust that the
moon will pull our subway in the right direction.

As in preservation of artifacts, plastic and sinew,
and this will be our garden of remnants,
durable, painted only as precursors to more temporary music.

As in accidents on the beach, sticky with ships and warnings
to vanishing lovers, of kites and habitat, knowing it all once
took place on a violin fingerboard where a hand moves up
and down from one position to another, looking for
something it has dropped;

we recognize it for a flash before it is gone again to a
ticking metronome.

Shift,

as in you had a meadow, an island,
a carnival of animals,
this duration of gifts for you, an ending
in songs of everything at once.

Shift,

> to be temporary and tolerated
> to be everything in a moment
> to be human and unfantastic

Acknowledgements

These poems, at times in different form or under different title, appeared as follows:

"Homeless," "Habitual Pasture as (Thoughts for Sad Times)," "Snowglobe" - *Requited Journal*

"Indigenous" - *Broadsided Press* & *Biggar Poetry Garden*

"Concerto Grosso op. 6, no. 4", 32" - *322 Review*

"In Love" (as "Poem for a Husband") - *Barge Press*

"Sunday Morning" - *As It Ought To Be* & *Assaracus*

"Sleep Therapy," "Technicolor," "Delicate Aches," "Travelogue" - *Assaracus*

About the Poet

Nicolas Destino, originally from Niagara Falls, New York, is a poet and essayist whose work includes a co-authored chapbook, *Of Kingdoms & Kangaroo*, and an essay, "Travel of Sound," which received notable mention in the *Best American Essays* series. He studied violin performance at SUNY Fredonia and received an MFA in poetry from Goddard College. Destino currently lives in Montclair, New Jersey, and teaches English at The College of New Rochelle in New York.

About the Press

Founded in 2010, Sibling Rivalry Press is an independent publishing house based in Alexander, Arkansas. Our mission is to develop, promote, and market underground artistic talent – those who don't quite fit into the mainstream. We are proud to be the home to *Assaracus*, the world's only print journal of gay male poetry. Our titles have been honored by the American Library Association through inclusion on its annual "Over the Rainbow" list of recommended LGBT reading and by *Library Journal*, who named *Assaracus* as a best new magazine of 2011. While we champion our LGBTIQ authors and artists, we are an inclusive publishing house and welcome all authors, artists, and readers regardless of sexual orientation or identity. [www.siblingrivalrypress.com]

CPSIA information can be obtained at www.ICGtesting.com
Printed in the USA
BVOW010215220113

311037BV00008B/31/P